BASKETBALL HALL OF **FAMERS**

KAREEM ABDUL-JABBAR

Martha Kneib

rosen central

To Todd, for everything

Published in 2002 by The Rosen Publishing Group, Inc.
29 East 21st Street, New York, NY 10010

Copyright © 2002 by The Rosen Publishing Group, Inc.

First Edition

Library of Congress Cataloging-in-Publication Data

Kneib, Martha.
Kareem Abdul-Jabbar / by Martha Kneib.
p. cm. — (Basketball Hall of Famers)
Includes bibliographical references and index.
Summary: Profiles the life and achievements of the twenty-year veteran player for the NBA.
ISBN 0-8239-3483-7 (lib. bdg.)
1. Abdul-Jabbar, Kareem, 1947-—Juvenile literature. 2. Basketball players—United States—Biography—Juvenile literature. [1. Abdul-Jabbar, Kareem, 1947- 2. Basketball players. 3. African Americans—Biography.] I. Title. II. Series.
GV884.A24 K54 2001
796.323'092—dc21

2001004189

Manufactured in the United States of America

contents

K areem Abdul-Jabbar is still an active basketball player. Although his time as a professional athlete has passed—he made history as a center for both the Milwaukee Bucks and the Los Angeles Lakers—this National Basketball Association (NBA) champ is applying his love of the sport to enrich the lives of young people.

Although many basketball players have been selected to the Basketball Hall of Fame since 1959, few have played as many seasons as Jabbar, a twenty-year NBA veteran. Jabbar is still involved with basketball, although as a coach rather than a player. His signature shot, the skyhook, has long gone rusty, but the hall of famer is now using his wisdom of a lifetime on the court to educate others.

UCLA center Lew Alcindor (now Kareem Abdul-Jabbar) leaps to rebound the ball during a college basketball game in 1969.

Jabbar was excellent for all of his twenty seasons in the NBA, but it takes more than good moves to be a superstar. Rising to the top takes talent and an overwhelming drive to excel. Jabbar had both, even before he was drafted to play professionally. This combination helped turn him from a great player into one of the best ever. However, he is not only one of the best athletes—Jabbar is also a person of high moral standards.

Throughout his life, Jabbar has used his interest in sports as a method to communicate with young people—including a turn as an assistant coach to an Apache high school team from 1998 to 1999. Off the court, he has raised money for various children's charities, such as Kareem's Kids, which he founded to motivate children to stay in school. He has also been involved with assorted literacy groups. Jabbar lent his support to projects that document the historical accomplishments of early African Americans, including a recent television film about civil rights activist Vernon Johns, and telling his own story in his autobiography *Giant Steps*. He is often quoted as saying that his reason for writing was because he felt that children were in need of positive and accessible role models.

Jabbar's advice to young people often echoes the wisdom in the pages of his book *Black Profiles in Courage*: "I define courage as recognizing when something needs to be done and doing it, even when there are easier choices. To me, that's the true measure of character."

It's certainly not easy to live up to Jabbar's definition of courage, even for him. It is also difficult to be both a famous athlete and a hero. Still, all obstacles aside, Kareem Abdul-Jabbar is both.

New York City

Kareem Abdul-Jabbar was born Ferdinand Lewis Alcindor Jr. on April 16, 1947, in New York City. He was the only child of his parents, Cora and Ferdinand "Al" Alcindor Sr., strict Catholics who lived in a section of New York City called Harlem. The Alcindor family had moved to New York City from Trinidad, which is an island nation in the Caribbean.

Lew, as he was called then, was a large infant—almost thirteen pounds. But because he came from a family of very tall people (his father was six feet three inches, and his mother was almost six feet tall), it was no surprise that he was going to be tall, too.

Jabbar's family was well educated. His father became bilingual because his job brought him into contact with many different people. Education was very important to the Alcindors, and they made sure Jabbar understood the importance of earning good grades from an early age. His parents expected him to be able to read well, long before his peers even began learning.

Jabbar's parents were very active in their faith and encouraged their son to have strong religious beliefs, too. They attended church regularly; in fact, they had met each other in a church choir. Jabbar's parents taught him the importance of strong family values. He later wrote about this in *Black Profiles in Courage*, "Like other youngsters, every so often I needed some outside guidance. I always looked to my family first. The most important lesson they taught me was the value of developing character . . . pride, honor, discipline, dignity, and courage of conviction and moral backbone."

Music also was a very important pastime in the Alcindor household. Jabbar's father, Al, went to the Juilliard School, which has a famous music division, in New York City. Al played the trombone and studied to be a conductor, a person who leads an orchestra. But when Al could not find work as a conductor, he worked for a furniture company instead. Later, he worked for the transit police, helping to protect people who ride on city buses and subways.

When Jabbar was just a few years old, his parents moved from Harlem to Inwood, a section of the city just north of Harlem. The neighborhood was filled with people who had come from many different places. Some were from countries in the Caribbean, such as Puerto Rico and Cuba. Others were from countries in Europe, such as Germany and Russia. As a result, Jabbar was influenced by a wide variety of different languages and cultures while growing up there.

Jabbar's parents were devout Catholics, and they sent their son to a Catholic school. By first grade he was enrolled in St. Jude's, a Catholic grammar school run by nuns. When Jabbar reached the third grade, he began to realize that he was the only African American student in his class. When he saw his class picture, he was surprised. As he recounted later in his autobiography *Giant Steps*, "I'm dark [skinned] and everybody else is light [skinned]!" Since he had always lived around people of all colors, he hadn't noticed the difference. Now, however, it was obvious. "I was darker than the rest of these kids. I didn't mention it to my parents when I got home that afternoon. I just had this special bit of information, and I tucked it away."

Away from Home

Jabbar remained enrolled at St. Jude's until the fourth grade. At that time, his parents decided it would be best for him to go to a boarding school where he would live full-time. The school was Holy Providence in Philadelphia. He disliked the boarding school

Fans watch as Jabbar moves to block an opponent's shot during a high school basketball game.

environment and was sometimes teased for being an excellent student. Other times, the abuse became physical.

Athletics, and especially basketball, quickly became a refuge for Jabbar, who had become a troubled student. "The only place I was even slightly safe was on the basketball court. Since I was the second tallest guy in the school, I was automatically on the team," he wrote in *Giant*

Steps. Jabbar wasn't very good yet, but the game was the only high point during his long school days. Instead of quitting because he couldn't play well, he worked very hard to learn the game.

Because he longed to be at home, Jabbar was sent back to St. Jude's when he reached the fifth grade. By then he was so tall that he was put on the school's eighth-grade basketball team, even though his size continued to make him feel awkward. Jabbar also became interested in running, so he joined the school's track team. This helped him develop his style on the basketball court.

As a seventh grader, Jabbar was six feet five inches tall and still growing. He was less awkward now, and he was making an attempt to become more agile. He learned to jump high enough to reach the edge of the basketball rim, and after a while, he could reach it many times in a row.

The hours spent on the basketball court were beginning to show in Jabbar's athletic performance. By the time he reached the eighth grade, he was a more confident player and much less awkward. In one game alone, he scored 33 points, a standout accomplishment for even a professional player. By this time he had grown to be six feet eight inches tall.

An Early Star Style

When Jabbar reached the age of fourteen, he could dunk the basketball—a move where players jump so high that their hand and the ball are both above the basket before the ball is pushed through the netting. Usually, players have to be very tall and have strong legs to dunk the ball. Most young athletes could never attempt this move, but Jabbar could do it well.

Because he was the tallest, his coach naturally put him in the center position. The center player not only jumps for the ball at the beginning of the game, but is also responsible for working close to the basket. In this way, the player in the center position can take passes from teammates, can make shots, and, if another teammate shoots and misses, he can control any rebound shots. While playing defensively, the center player stays near the other team's center and tries to block potential shots. Jabbar played poorly at first, but because he was driven to excel in his newfound position, he practiced constantly.

Even though Jabbar was busy with basketball, his parents did not allow him to neglect his schoolwork. Because he was a good student, and great on the court, several high schools wanted him to enroll and play on their basketball team. Jabbar met the basketball coach of Power Memorial Academy, Jack Donohue, and liked him a great deal. He began attending classes and playing basketball for Power Memorial in the fall of 1961.

Powerful, but Awkward

Jabbar didn't fit in very well and spent much of his time by himself. He was an only child, and he was quite used to being alone. Jabbar's parents also kept him sheltered from anyone they thought might be a bad influence. He resorted to playing basketball, a sport that he could practice alone anytime that he wanted.

The time he spent practicing was beginning to show itself in his playing skill. He was becoming more and more graceful. He worked very hard during the summer breaks and kept improving his game while playing alone on the courts every day, sometimes all day.

During Jabbar's sophomore year, he made the varsity team at Power Memorial. Coach Donohue, who was dedicated to his team, trained along with his students and inspired them to do their best. Donohue helped Jabbar develop his game until he understood the sport of basketball more than he ever had before. In fact, Jabbar led his teammates through that season with no losses.

Since Power Memorial did not have a tradition of successful basketball teams, most people never came to see its team play. As the team won game after game, however, more people came to the gym to see Jabbar and his teammates.

Kareem Abdul-Jabbar attempts a jump shot during a high school basketball game at Madison Square Garden in 1963.

This pressure was difficult in the beginning. He felt as if all the people watching would be unhappy if the team lost. He felt personally responsible for the outcome of each game.

That year, Power Memorial's success frustrated their opponents. During one game, an opposing player assaulted Jabbar by attempting to bite him. That player was thrown out of the game, but the animosity between Jabbar and his opponents continued.

Now that Power Memorial had a winning team, many reporters wanted to talk to Jabbar, but Donohue wouldn't let him speak with reporters. Donohue wanted Jabbar to focus only on basketball and schoolwork, without the additional stress of becoming a local newspaper favorite. It was also important to Donohue that team members act like a team, without singling out the skills of one player. Jabbar took these lessons to heart and learned the value of being a team member.

After their regular season, the Power Memorial team went on to win the city championship, and Jabbar was chosen all-city and all-American. He was very pleased to be noticed while in high school. He liked basketball, and having those honors just made the sport that much more fun.

Occasionally, Donohue would get tickets to professional basketball games at Madison Square Garden in New York City, and he and Jabbar would go and watch games played by great players such as Wilt Chamberlain, Bill Russell, and Bob Cousy. "I wasn't even thinking about playing professional ball," he said in *Giant Steps.* "I just wanted to pick up some pointers. I learned how to use the outlet pass from watching Bill Russell."

For the second season in a row, Power Memorial won every game, including the city championship, though a few of the games were close calls. Jabbar was again chosen all-city and all-American, and the team seemed unbeatable.

Black Culture and Civil Rights

During the summer after his junior year, Jabbar applied for a position with the Harlem Youth

Action Project. He got a job in a journalism workshop, where he learned basic writing skills and how to be a good reporter. Most of the assignments were about the other areas of the organization, such as the drama, music, and dance workshops. Other times, the reporters wrote about current events in New York City.

While researching local architecture, Jabbar discovered the Schomburg Center for Research in Black Culture. He found many fascinating things at the center. He learned about the Jazz Age in Harlem in the 1920s, when African American artists and intellectuals— musicians, dancers, painters, and writers—all thrived together and created some of the most valued art of the century. This period of artistic growth is sometimes referred to as the Harlem Renaissance. It echoed the insights of many famous people, such as W. E. B. Du Bois, a civil rights activist and the first African American to receive a Ph.D. from Harvard University. Jabbar also learned about the poet Langston Hughes and the novelist Ralph Ellison.

The Schomburg Center for Research in Black Culture *(right)* is shown with the original Schomburg Center Building *(left)*, where Jabbar learned about the Harlem Renaissance and about African American history in general.

Learning about Harlem's past excited Jabbar because he had lived in Harlem during his boyhood. He had developed a sense of pride and respect for himself and for his community. He had also developed an interest in civil rights. He went to hear Dr. Martin Luther King Jr. speak in New York City. He can even be seen in the background of photos taken of Dr. King, the famed Baptist minister who was committed to

Reading about historical African American leaders like W. E. B. Du Bois *(above)* spurred Jabbar's interest in the Civil Rights movement.

nonviolence and was later assassinated for his convictions. Jabbar became even more interested in issues like racism and African American culture, though he didn't necessarily always agree with Dr. King. "I didn't subscribe to his philosophy of nonviolence," he recounted in his book *Kareem*. "In retrospect, though, I've come to realize that his way is probably the only way."

Race Riots

One summer night in July 1964, Jabbar stepped out of the subway and into a riot. He had heard the sound of gunfire and watched people smash things in the street. Fire leaped from some buildings' windows. Jabbar had been a reporter for several weeks, and he thought briefly about trying to write about what he saw that night. He quickly realized he was in too much danger and ran away as fast as he could.

Over the next few days, Jabbar did some research. Two days before the riot, a white policeman had shot and killed an African American high school student. The student was unarmed, but the policeman thought he had a gun. The people in Harlem didn't believe the policeman's story about seeing a gun, and they were angry. Their rioting was a call for justice in the wake of the student's death. Jabbar reported on the five days of riots, and he was angry, too. He felt, like many other people in Harlem, that the police worked against the people they were supposed to protect.

A week after the riots, Jabbar went to Friendship Farm, a basketball camp north of New York City, to help Coach Donohue educate youngsters about basketball, since he enjoyed helping children. He had gone to the camp the year before. This season, however, he was distracted. He couldn't stop thinking about the riots and about Harlem. Although he had grown up around people of all races, he began to feel more and more anger toward whites. He couldn't wait to get away from the farm's peaceful summer setting and return to Inwood.

Back to School

In the fall of 1964, Jabbar returned to Power Memorial for his senior year. Again, the basketball team had a dynamic and winning season before succumbing in their final game to a powerful Maryland high school with a score of 43–46. Power Memorial had finally lost, but their winning streak stood proud at a total of seventy-one games. For a high school that had never had a winning team before, it was a very exciting time. For a third consecutive year, Jabbar was voted all-city and all-American.

With the basketball season over and his senior year winding down, Jabbar had to decide where he would go to college. After much thought, he narrowed his choices to four schools: St. John's University, Columbia University, the University of Michigan, and the University of California at Los Angeles (UCLA).

Jabbar wanted to leave home and gain some independence from his parents. Like many other teenagers, he wanted to be considered an adult. For that reason, he was most interested in schools far away from New York City.

He visited UCLA and was impressed with its beautiful, pristine campus. People were friendly, and the weather was warm. Also, they had a great team. UCLA had won two national championships in the early 1960s. The team even had a new place to play basketball: the Pauley Pavilion.

Best of all, UCLA employed Coach John Wooden. Jabbar met with him when he visited the campus and felt that he had a strong sense of dignity and inner courage. Wooden had been inducted as a player into the Basketball Hall of Fame in 1961, but in 1973, he was also

Opponents struggle to defend against
the much taller Kareem Abdul-
Jabbar during the Catholic High
School Championships in New York.

inducted as a coach—one of only two people to have that honor!

Wooden had all of the characteristics of a talented college coach: courage, talent, and drive, capped by a great professional career. Jabbar wanted to play basketball for him because he knew Wooden would help him achieve his goals to play professional basketball. As a result, UCLA was Jabbar's college choice.

On his final morning in New York, he took several pictures of his home, his friends, and his parents—everyone and everything he knew he would miss. But Jabbar was excited about UCLA and his first chance to live away from home. He finished taking the pictures, kissed his parents good-bye, and headed for California and his dream.

Los Angeles:
The College Years

Jabbar enjoyed being a freshman at UCLA, though he went through periods of culture shock. California, with its warm sun and cool surf, was very different from New York, with its moody temperament and gray, polluted haze. People were so friendly that sometimes he thought that everyone wanted to find a way to meet "the new basketball player from New York." Because he was accustomed to being alone, the attention he received on campus and on the court wore thin very quickly. Soon he found himself avoiding people whenever he could.

Jabbar found his school writing assignments easy after working as a reporter. In one class he wrote a paper on the famous jazz club the Village

Vanguard, and his essay was selected to be read to the class. He was pleased that his writing was so well received and realized that his academic training, both at home and at school, had prepared him well.

During his first year, Jabbar played on UCLA's freshman basketball team. Coach Wooden asked a man named Jay Carty to come to UCLA to help Jabbar learn how to expand his skills. Carty and Jabbar played a lot of one-on-one. Carty also had him jump up to touch a line eighteen inches above the basketball rim, and Jabbar practiced this action twenty times with each hand, every day.

The tiring schedule of school and athletics often exhausted Jabbar. One reason was that he was still growing. While he was attending UCLA, he grew from seven feet to seven feet two inches. Most people have stopped growing by the time they go to college, but Jabbar just kept getting taller.

He also worked very hard on his hook shot. Carty encouraged Jabbar to work at

The UCLA Bruins center seems to float through the air as he rebounds the ball during an NCAA game in 1967.

rebounds and agility drills. All the practice helped him develop the shot that would one day become his trademark: the skyhook. The skyhook was an elevated hook shot that would seem to float in the air, then sink right into the net. Jabbar made the shot while his back was to the man guarding him. Since his body protected the ball and because he jumped so high, his opponents could not stop him from scoring. It became Jabbar's signature shot—no one else in college or the pros had one like it. No one else has had one like it since.

During his first year, the freshman basketball team played the varsity players, a team that was ranked number one in the country. A big crowd of people turned out for the first game played in Pauley Pavilion, and they were surprised by the space and the outcome: The freshman team won by a margin of 15 points!

Jabbar scored 31 points. The freshman team won partly because the varsity team did not have anyone who could guard Jabbar. He

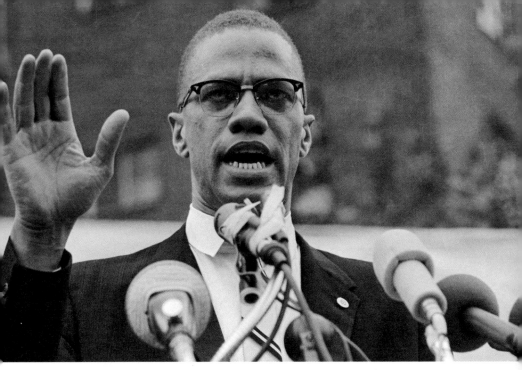

African American leader Malcolm X. Kareem Abdul-Jabbar began considering conversion to Islam after reading *The Autobiography of Malcolm X.*

was too skilled. If he got the ball, he could score. If the varsity team sent two men to guard him, he passed the ball to one of his teammates who was open and could also shoot. Jabbar made good use of the lessons he had learned about teamwork. If he couldn't score, he got the ball to another teammate who could. Not only did the freshman team win against the varsity team, they also won every game that season with a simple strategy: No one could beat Jabbar.

The Influence of Malcolm X

Jabbar was just as enthusiastic about his studies. During his freshman year, he read *The Autobiography of Malcolm X.* An outspoken African American leader, Malcolm X preached against racism in the United States and across the globe.

Jabbar found the story of Malcolm X's life very exciting. Malcolm X's mother was from the Caribbean, just like his own parents, and Malcolm X had also lived in Harlem. Jabbar was interested in this man who had traveled paths quite similar to his own.

But Malcolm X's autobiography touched Jabbar in another way, too. The civil rights activist had converted to the religion of Islam. He had become a Muslim, and this had changed his ideas about life. Through Islam, Malcolm X came to understand that all people were equal. He realized that some people were good and some were bad, but their goodness did not depend on their race. It was what people felt inside that made the difference. In his autobiography,

Malcolm X told the story about meeting a white man who asked, "Do you mind shaking hands with a white man?" Malcolm X said, "I don't mind shaking hands with human beings."

Jabbar thought carefully about how he should treat other people. He hadn't liked the ways in which others had treated him in his life because of his ethnicity. After the 1964 riot in Harlem, he had internalized a great anger toward white people. Even after reading Malcolm X's autobiography, Jabbar wasn't certain he could defend his anger or release it.

UCLA Varsity Basketball

The following year, Jabbar became a sophomore and began to play on UCLA's varsity team. Since two of the senior players had left, Wooden now had a varsity team of one junior and four sophomores, unusual for any college varsity team. Wooden, however, did not have a choice. He made the sophomores, including Jabbar, work very hard because they had to play against seniors with much more experience. If they weren't careful, UCLA's lack of skill would cost them dearly.

In one early game of the season, the team played against the University of Southern California (USC), and Jabbar scored 56 points, a UCLA record. In the following game, three men were assigned to guard Jabbar, so he only scored 19 points. But Jabbar knew the value of teamwork and used the opportunity to pass the ball to his teammates. They scored easily, and UCLA won again. As he said in his book *Kareem*, he was "more hungry for the win than for glory."

UCLA's efforts were effective. They went undefeated that season, unchallenged by any other team. Winning every contest also meant that UCLA went to the National Collegiate Athletic Association (NCAA) Tournament, where they became champions.

During the summer after winning the NCAA Tournament, Jabbar went back to New York and worked for the New York City Housing Authority, teaching children how to play basketball. He loved being able to show them how to understand the strategies of the game. Jabbar didn't earn much money, but felt that he was making a difference in the lives of the young people he met.

In the fall of 1967, Jabbar returned to UCLA for his junior year. Since the university had not lost a game the previous year, he and his teammates knew every team would want to beat them.

Jabbar had other obstacles, too. The College Basketball Rules Committee had changed the rules over the summer and now it was illegal to dunk the ball—one of Jabbar's best moves. He now had to learn to use different shots. Although he didn't like it at the time, learning new shots was essential. Later during his career, he would employ a variety of shots to earn points.

An eye injury kept Jabbar off the court for several games that season, and UCLA felt his absence. He stayed in the hospital for three days with blurry vision before he played a game against the University of Houston. Jabbar was tired and couldn't see very well. Even so, UCLA lost the game by only 2 points.

Kareem Abdul-Jabbar (pictured near the backboard) celebrates winning the 1967 NCAA championship with his UCLA Bruins teammates and coaches.

Eventually, both Jabbar and UCLA recovered and went on to win the season's remaining games. They went to the NCAA Tournament again to play the University of Houston in the semifinals. Everyone on UCLA's team was determined to win and bounce back. With Jabbar's determination, Houston never had a chance. UCLA won by 32 points. UCLA then beat North Carolina and won the tournament again, ending Jabbar's second varsity season just as splendidly as his first.

Jabbar Discovers Islamic Religion and Culture

Meanwhile, Jabbar was still immersed in his college studies and was now thinking about his spirituality. He wanted to find a religion that would help him live a good life and be a person of high moral character, but he didn't want to continue practicing catholicism like his parents. He studied other religions, but none felt appropriate. "Monotheism was still very much ingrained in me; it made sense to me that there

Kareem Abdul-Jabbar prays in a mosque in Jerusalem.

would be one very complex superior source
from which all the natural forces of the world
would flow," he said in *Giant Steps*.

Jabbar remembered feeling inspired by
what he had learned about Islam from Malcolm
X's autobiography. A friend suggested that he
read the Qur'an, a book of religious thought.
The Qur'an was written by the prophet
Muhammad in the seventh century AD. Muslims
believe it was dictated to Muhammad by an

angel sent by God. Muslims call god Allah. The Qur'an is like the Christian Bible; it details events and wisdom important to the Muslims.

One of the main ideals of the Qur'an is that all people are equal. Jabbar was still angry about the injustices that he saw in the world and wasn't sure if he agreed with that ideal. But most of what he learned from the Qur'an meant a great deal to him.

During the summer of 1968, Jabbar studied Islamic cultures and decided to become a Muslim. He went to a mosque (an Islamic place of worship and study) and asked to learn more about the religion.

Over the summer, Jabbar studied Islamic culture. He learned how to prepare for the Sabbath, or holy day, which is Friday for Muslims. He memorized passages from the Qur'an. After a month of study, Jabbar stood up in front of witnesses in the mosque and made his shahada. This is an Islamic rite of passage. It is done when someone asserts that he or she believes Allah is God and Muhammad is God's messenger. After completing his shahada, Jabbar was considered a Muslim.

Jabbar's teacher gave him a new Muslim name that was intended only for religious purposes. The teacher chose the names Abdul, meaning "servant of Allah," and Kareem, which means "generous." Jabbar didn't change his name anywhere except at the mosque where he prayed. He remained Lew Alcindor in school and on the basketball court. While at the mosque, he was called Abdul-Kareem.

Sometimes, this made Jabbar feel unsettled. He felt like Abdul-Kareem was now his real name, but he did not want to forget the name his parents gave him.

New Friends

That summer, Jabbar met a man who would become very important to him: Hamaas Abdul-Khaalis. Khaalis was a Muslim who lived in New York. He asked Jabbar about what he had been taught because he felt that his Islamic education was insufficient. When he asked Jabbar questions

Kareem Abdul-Jabbar makes his big screen debut in *Game of Death* (1978), a martial-arts film starring his good friend Bruce Lee.

about certain passages in the Qur'an, Jabbar did not know the answers.

As a result, Jabbar decided to learn more about Islam from Khaalis. Jabbar went to his house every morning at 6:00 AM for two hours of intensive studying before beginning work three hours later.

Khaalis taught Jabbar to judge others by how well they lived their lives and not to base any criticism on their ethnicity or skin color. He said that Jabbar should care about them if they were good people. These were the same ideas that were expressed in Malcolm X's autobiography. Now those ideas made more sense. Jabbar was ready to let go of his anger and rage. He believed it was an important lesson to learn. He realized that there are always some people from every group who will live without morals or values, but judging them based on the color of their skin was wrong.

Jabbar continually learned about Islamic customs. He could not drink alcohol or eat pork. He took his shoes off before entering someone's home. He learned that he should wash a certain way before praying. He prayed five times a day, facing east toward Mecca, the holiest city in Islam.

At the end of the summer, Khaalis thought Jabbar had learned enough to give him his shahada again. Afterward, Khaalis gave him a new name. Khaalis added Jabbar, which means "powerful," to the name he already had. Abdul-Kareem was now Kareem Abdul-Jabbar, at least during prayer and with his fellow Muslims.

It's easy to understand how Jabbar's hatred of racism introduced him to an Islamic world. Time and again he has said that being Muslim forces a person to understand the differences between what is morally right or wrong. He explained, "As a Muslim, when you make the wrong choice you are aware of it. It totally eliminates the possibility of being a hypocrite. You can't say, 'I was ignorant.' I think [my religious conversion] has done me a lot of good."

Finally, Jabbar told his parents about his conversion. At first, they were openly hostile. It took many years for them to overcome the hurt and division they felt within their family. Years later, his father, Al, recounted in the *New York Daily News*, that "we didn't approve, but that's what he wanted to do. Eventually, we came to terms with his decision."

Jabbar went back to UCLA for his senior year. This time, the team won every game except the final contest. Generally, time passed slowly, and Jabbar had a very lonely year. He didn't think basketball was fun anymore. And he didn't have many other Muslims with whom to communicate. He had changed the way he lived, but he had no one with whom to share his new ideas and beliefs. He didn't know anyone at UCLA who would understand his new name and religious devotion.

Then Jabbar met someone else who would become important to him: Bruce Lee. Lee had invented a new style of fighting. He was also a movie star and had been on the television series *The Green Hornet*. Jabbar learned some fighting skills from Lee. This was sometimes a problem for Lee because Jabbar was so tall! He could reach Lee before Lee could get close enough to Jabbar to hit him. By now, Jabbar was very agile, not at all awkward like he had been as a boy.

Jabbar and Lee became friends, which encouraged Jabbar during his last year at UCLA. Learning martial arts also helped him become even more polished on the court. The awkward boy from Inwood had a newfound grace.

Kareem Abdul-Jabbar wears the basket netting around his neck after leading UCLA to victory in the NCAA basketball championship in 1968.

UCLA won its third straight NCAA championship without missing a beat. Jabbar was selected the Most Outstanding Player for the third time in a row. The UCLA team broke the records with five consecutive NCAA titles, and for consecutive number of tournament games won. In short, the UCLA team had lost only two games out of the ninety they had played during the three years Jabbar was on the team.

He ended his wonderful college career as the top scorer in UCLA history.

But it was over. It was time to think about playing professionally. Jabbar wanted to go back to New York to be near his parents and Khaalis, but the local team there—the New York Knicks—did not win the right to draft him. Instead, the Milwaukee Bucks wanted Jabbar, so he signed a contract with that team. In June 1969, Jabbar graduated from UCLA and embarked on his NBA career.

3

Milwaukee

Jabbar signed with the Milwaukee Bucks without considering what life would be like in the small Wisconsin city. For one thing, the winters were very cold. Jabbar had lived through some severe winters in New York, but winters in Wisconsin were much worse. During his first winter in Milwaukee, the north window of his apartment became a solid sheet of ice.

Also, very few people in Milwaukee knew anything about Islam. Once again, Jabbar felt isolated. And, because he didn't make his religion public, he continued to live a double life. He was now Kareem Abdul-Jabbar, but people still called him Lew Alcindor in public and in the media.

Kareem Abdul-Jabbar, the Milwaukee Bucks center, prepares to pass the ball during an NBA game against the New York Knicks in 1972.

Milwaukee was much smaller than New York or Los Angeles, and Jabbar found it difficult to socialize. Because he was Muslim, he could not drink or gamble, which is what some of his teammates did off the court. Yet, even though he didn't fit into his new life in Milwaukee well, Jabbar was still liked by the Milwaukee fans. When he walked onto the court for rookie training camp, waiting fans gave him a standing ovation.

They were hoping Jabbar could help them win. The Bucks had played for only one season, and they limped through it. But now, with the talented kid from UCLA, they had higher hopes.

Because Jabbar had been so good in college, he discovered many people expected him to be even better when he became a professional player. Jabbar felt pressured to live up to their expectations, since they demanded perfection. While no one can live up to that expectation, Jabbar did his best.

While in college, Jabbar had played on teams using a zone defense. But in the pros, a zone defense was not allowed. Teams had to play man to man. Jabbar would guard one of the other team's forwards to be able to stay near the basket. That way, he could try to block the other team's shots. Jabbar's teammates could count on him to do his job so well that they would concentrate on other strategies, such as stealing the ball. If they failed and another player got to shoot the ball, Jabbar would be there to block the shot. The team started the season slowly but developed their teamwork over the course of the season's first half.

Jabbar also discovered that professional basketball was far more physically interactive than college basketball. The other team's players pushed him on the court, behavior that would never be allowed in college. Eventually Jabbar learned to handle this rougher style of play.

Life off the Court

After half a season, the Bucks really began to do well. As he said in *Kareem,* "We went from being the doormat of the league to being a very

Kareem tries to deny the Chicago
Bulls' Norm van Lier a clear
path to the basket during a
playoff game.

good team." The Bucks finished the season in second place in their division, which was an amazing feat considering they had done so poorly the year before.

The Bucks had lost to the New York Knicks in the NBA semifinals, but Jabbar had such a good season that he was named Rookie of the Year, an honor that made him very happy.

After the season, Jabbar went to Washington, D.C., to visit Khaalis, his Islam teacher who had moved there with his family and some students. Jabbar wanted to do something to help Khaalis as much as Khaalis had helped him. Khaalis had found a building where he could start a mosque and community center. Jabbar put the down payment on the building and offered to give it to his friend. Khaalis, however, did not want to own the building; instead, he wanted Jabbar to be able to sell it if he needed to.

The house remained Jabbar's property, but Khaalis and his family lived and worshiped there. Jabbar stopped by as often as he could to visit with fellow Muslims and to participate in the community's life. He also contributed money to the center.

Besides the Muslim community, Jabbar also spent money helping his parents. He wanted to make sure they had enough to live well. Jabbar's professional career helped give him the ability to live up to the meaning of his Islamic name Kareem, which means "generous."

Khaalis influenced Jabbar's life in many ways. Khaalis told Jabbar that a Muslim man should be married. Jabbar liked a woman who had joined Khaalis's group. Her name had been Janice Brown, but Khaalis had renamed her Habiba after her conversion to Islam. Jabbar had met Habiba, but he didn't have time to get to know her before it was time to go back to Milwaukee, so his interest in her waned.

Building Momentum

During the next season, Jabbar played very well and was helped by another player. The Bucks had signed Oscar Robertson, known to many as the Big O, to play on their team. Robertson was a great all-around basketball player. He was six feet five inches—nine inches shorter than Jabbar—but he was not a center, he was a guard, a position where height is less important. Robertson was an excellent passer, rebounder, and scorer. Though older than Jabbar and closer to retirement, Robertson was still one of the most talented players in the league.

One thing that Robertson did very well was make assists. That meant he passed the ball to other players to score. Also, if Robertson couldn't pass, Jabbar could attempt to block a player and allow Robertson a clearer shot. Robertson could score quite often if given the opportunity, and both players worked well together.

For the first time in his career, Jabbar played against his boyhood hero, Wilt Chamberlain. Although Chamberlain had been injured during Jabbar's rookie year, the two centers were now both on the court for the full season. Chamberlain was known as the top

Kareem Abdul-Jabbar gropes helplessly as the Los Angeles Lakers' Wilt Chamberlain slaps away his hook shot during a 1972 NBA playoff game.

center in basketball, but when he and Jabbar went up against each other, Jabbar held his own. It would not take long for Jabbar to replace Chamberlain as the best player in the center position.

By the end of the season, the Bucks went to the playoffs. They were only in their third year as a team, and, as an expansion team, they were expected to fail. With Jabbar, however, the Bucks had gone from the basement to the Finals of the NBA championships in only two seasons.

In the championship game, the Bucks faced the Baltimore Bullets, who had won the right to be in the Finals by beating the New York Knicks. The Knicks had taken the Bucks out of the playoffs the year before, and the Bucks had been hoping for a payback. Instead, they played Baltimore.

Jabbar and the rest of the Bucks were so hungry for the championship that they swept the Bullets in just four games, giving Jabbar a championship after only two seasons in the league! He was overjoyed. Then Jabbar was

Jabbar enters the car he received for winning the 1971 MVP award outside the famed Mama Leone's Restaurant in New York City on May 6, 1971.

named the NBA's Most Valuable Player (MVP) for the season. Having both honors was a highlight in Jabbar's life. He was so happy he could barely think of anything else.

The summer after the winning 1970–1971 season, Jabbar married Habiba at the building he had bought for Khaalis to use as a mosque. Then he decided that it was time for another big change. That fall, Jabbar legally changed his name from Ferdinand Lewis Alcindor Jr. to

Kareem Abdul-Jabbar. He would no longer live a double life. From now on, everyone would know that he wanted to live his life as a Muslim.

During the next basketball season, Jabbar had a difficult time making everyone understand he had a new name. Many people still called him Lew. But he persisted, and soon everyone remembered and respected his choice.

By the end of the next season, Jabbar and the Bucks were in the NBA division playoffs, but they lost to the Los Angeles Lakers. For the second time in a row, he was chosen to be the league's MVP. His disappointment over their loss was so great, though, that the honor couldn't lift his spirits.

Kareem and Habiba welcomed their daughter, who was also named Habiba, three weeks after the season ended. In Islam, it is customary to pray the adhan at a baby's birth. The adhan is a prayer that praises Allah. Kareem prayed the adhan while holding his newborn daughter and felt the emptiness in his heart lift completely. He could not know it at that moment, but his joy would only be temporary.

Tragedy Strikes

In January 1973, Jabbar received terrible news. Some men went to the house he had bought for Khaalis and had killed several people, including some of Khaalis's children. The men had intended to kill Khaalis, but when they found he wasn't at home, they shot whoever was there. Many people who weren't at the house were threatened, even Jabbar. Everywhere he went, Jabbar had a police escort.

Jabbar was devastated. He fled the country and traveled around the world, including North Africa, where many Muslims lived. He had taken a course in Arabic at Harvard University the year before, and now he was finally able to use some of the knowledge he'd learned. He enjoyed speaking Arabic when he could, and learned about the traditions of different cultures.

Despite his journey, that year continued to be a tragic one. While he was out of the country, he heard that his old friend and martial arts teacher, Bruce Lee, had died. Jabbar had filmed a few scenes in a movie called *Game of Death* with Lee, and he had hoped to see him again. Now he would never get that chance.

When he returned to life in Milwaukee, he realized that he and Habiba weren't happy together. They discussed their marriage and decided to separate. Habiba went to Washington, D.C., to be with Khaalis's community, and Jabbar remained in Milwaukee.

Those Championship Bucks

Instead of being sad, Jabbar put all his energy into his basketball career. Oscar "the Big O" Robertson still played for the Bucks, and the team had a talented bench to call on when someone fouled out or needed to rest. With no weaknesses in any position, the Bucks won game after game. By the end of the season, they had the best record in the league.

The Bucks had beaten the Lakers and the Chicago Bulls to face the Boston Celtics in the

NBA Finals in 1974. Both teams battled very intensely. Game 6 was tied at the end of regulation play and went into overtime. With only seven seconds to go, the Celtics were ahead by one point. The Bucks had one chance to tie it again, and Jabbar hooked the ball right into the basket. Now the game went into double overtime! The Bucks remained focused and won the match by one point, causing much excitement and a sleepless night for Jabbar.

The sixth game had been exciting, but the Bucks still needed to win Game 7. The Bucks lost that game to the Celtics, leaving Jabbar without an NBA championship yet again.

The next season did not go well for the Bucks either. Oscar Robertson retired, several players were traded, and Jabbar was injured. He broke a bone in his hand, and another player gouged him in the eye. The Bucks finished last in their division. Jabbar felt depressed. He had never played on a losing team before. His eye and hand healed, but too slowly for him to help his team win.

After this second eye injury, Jabbar began wearing protective goggles during all games.

Jabbar decided it was time to leave Milwaukee. He was not happy, even though his fans remained faithful. They showed up when the team was winning and when they were losing. Best of all, they always cheered the players they liked, and they liked Jabbar. It was the fans that had kept him in Milwaukee for so long, but now it was time to go. The Bucks agreed to trade him, and Jabbar would play for the Los Angeles Lakers during the 1975–1976 season.

Los Angeles: The Laker Years

Jabbar felt happy to be back in Los Angeles, a city where he felt grounded. That season was both good and bad for the future Hall of Famer. He had one of the best seasons of his career. He had led the league in rebounds and blocked shots, was second in scoring, and was chosen as MVP for the fourth time. However, basketball is a team sport, and Jabbar was only one player. He couldn't make up for a lack of talent in other positions. Jabbar was hot, but the team finished fourth in the division. Joining the Lakers had not been enough for Jabbar to get on a winning team.

The next season, the Lakers fared better. They made it to the playoffs, but two of their players were injured. The Portland Trail Blazers beat them again, but this time in four consecutive games.

A Second Marriage and a New Image

It was around this time that Jabbar met the woman who would, in 1979, become his second wife, Cheryl Pistano. She helped him see how much he had closed himself off from other people and how cynical he'd become as a result of his forced isolation. In his book *Giant Steps*, Jabbar recounted how, on their first date, he told Cheryl about his life. "I dribble a ball up and down a court—if you could consider that a job."

Jabbar had never liked being asked for autographs because he felt that only pests would interrupt his day to ask him to sign something. Cheryl helped him realize that fans who asked for autographs were doing so because they admired him. They appreciated the way he played basketball. She told Jabbar it was an insult to ignore people who were trying to express their admiration. Jabbar changed his mind about his fans. He learned to appreciate that most of them were people who wanted to show him their loyalty and affection.

During the 1978–1979 season, Jabbar was pleased that the Lakers chose him to be their captain. The Lakers didn't have much talent in their forwards, though, so they had a difficult time. They finished the season in third place, and no one expected them to pass the first round of the playoffs. Despite everyone's low expectations of them, the Lakers beat the Denver Nuggets 112–111. They lost to the Seattle Supersonics in the next round, but they had proven that they could still win.

Jabbar was depressed over the loss, but then something wonderful happened. A television sportscaster named Ted Dawson asked people to send Jabbar and the Lakers telegrams to tell them how much they were appreciated. Within days, the mail started piling up in stacks. The support from the fans

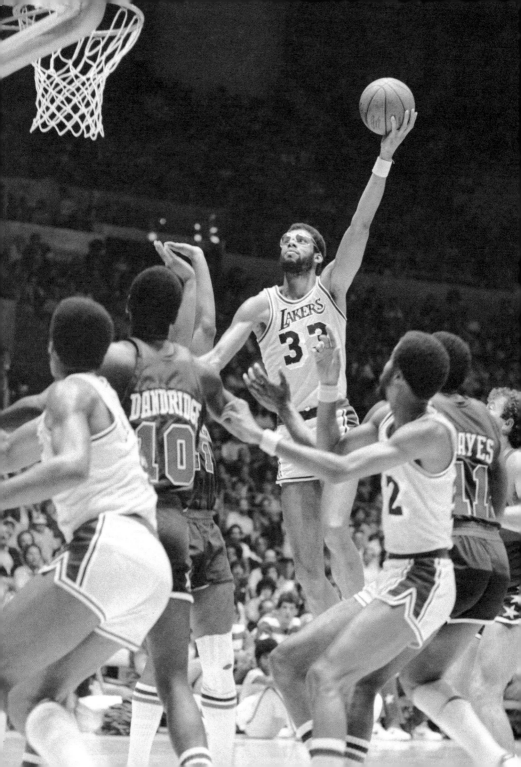

meant so much to Jabbar that he kept every letter. Years later, he still had them.

In an effort to brighten his image, Jabbar did more interviews. He tried to offer more of himself because he realized now that people really liked him. One night he looked right into the camera during an interview and said, "Hi to Mom and Pops in New York!" The reaction was incredible. Everyone loved the fact that Jabbar had acknowledged his parents and his home city.

The next season promised to be even better. Earvin "Magic" Johnson was drafted to be on the team, and two strong forwards had also been signed. The new owner had personally negotiated Jabbar's new contract, which Jabbar took as a sign of respect. He felt much more positive about the Lakers.

The team had a great season and finished first in their division, but Jabbar was eager for another championship. It had been several years since he had been on a winning team, and he wanted to hold the NBA title again.

Jabbar moves to deliver the skyhook in a game against the Washington Bullets on October 30, 1978.

The Lakers and the Philadelphia 76ers split the first four games in the series. During Game 5, Jabbar was injured. The team doctor asked him if he wanted to go to the hospital right away, but Jabbar had the doctor tape up his ankle instead. He went back out on the court and continued playing. His ankle hurt him badly, so much that he couldn't jump. Even in pain, Jabbar went on to score 40 points and won the game by 5 before heading to the local hospital for X rays. Shortly after, unsurprisingly, he was again voted the league's MVP.

Jabbar missed the final two games while recuperating at home. But the Lakers won. Jabbar didn't like missing the games and victories with the team, but finally he was on a championship team again.

He took some time during the off-season to act in the movie *Airplane*, in which he played the part of Roger the copilot. The movie's success made him even more recognizable to people—even those who weren't interested in sports. Everything seemed to be wonderful. The Lakers were on the top of their game, and they had another championship win two seasons later, with Jabbar there to celebrate. When the next season started, they looked hot. Jabbar looked forward to another winning season and another possible championship.

Fire!

Then, tragedy struck. While Jabbar was on the road, his house caught on fire. Cheryl and their son, Amir, were home when she awakened to find the house consumed in flames. Fortunately, everyone got out safely. However, everything Jabbar owned was destroyed. His collection of jazz albums had melted. His four Qur'ans from the Middle Ages were now a pile of ash. Lovely pieces of art he had carefully selected over the years had been incinerated. Fire and smoke had destroyed a lifetime of photographs, belongings, and clothing.

Kareem Abdul-Jabbar as Roger the copilot in *Airplane*.

Jabbar was shocked. "I would think about reading a book, or listening to an album, or putting on a favorite shirt, and they'd be gone," he said in *Giant Steps*. His world had turned upside down.

Now Jabbar had another opportunity to realize how much he meant to other people. A radio station sent him 1,500 jazz albums to help replace his collection. Many people from around the United States sent Jabbar gifts and good wishes. He was grateful to all the people who showed their support and was surprised, once again, to find that his fans cared.

An Uncertain Future

By 1985, some people were claiming that Jabbar, now almost forty, was too old to play the game. During the season Finals, the Lakers met the Celtics and were defeated in the first game of the series with a final score of 148–114. People thought the Lakers were spent, but Jabbar took it upon himself to change those opinions.

First, he spoke to everyone at the team meeting and apologized. He said he hadn't done as well as he could have and he would do better in the second game. He was so calm and determined that the rest of his teammates took heart. In the second game, he scored 30 points and blocked an important shot by one of the Celtics with only four minutes left in the game. He also broke the record for most points scored in the playoffs by a single player. As a result, the Lakers won the game by 7 points.

The Lakers also won the third game with Jabbar scoring 26 points. Though the team lost the fourth game to the Celtics, they won Game 5.

The final game was played at the Celtics' home court in Boston, so most fans believed that their win was certain. But Jabbar scored 18 points in the second half, and the Lakers won by 11 points. Afterward, a joyful Jabbar surprised everyone. He sprayed his teammates with champagne to celebrate the well-deserved title.

Laker Day!

When the team returned to Los Angeles, they were greeted by a welcome parade. The mayor of Los Angeles declared the day of the parade to be Laker Day. Everyone was thrilled that the home team had won and was overjoyed when Jabbar was named the MVP of the tournament. For Jabbar, the end of the 1984–1985 season was one of the highlights of his long career.

The 1988–1989 season was Jabbar's last year of professional play. As he said in his book *Kareem*, "I never thought when I started out that I would end up playing basketball longer than anyone has ever played the game before. I can remember, very keenly, being a rookie and wondering what guys did after playing professional ball for ten years." After twenty years, Jabbar finally had to figure it out for himself.

Even though some people wanted him to leave even earlier because of his injuries,

Kareem Abdul-Jabbar *(center, with goggles)* hooks the ball over the Detroit Pistons' Bill Laimbeer as Magic Johnson *(number 32)* looks on.

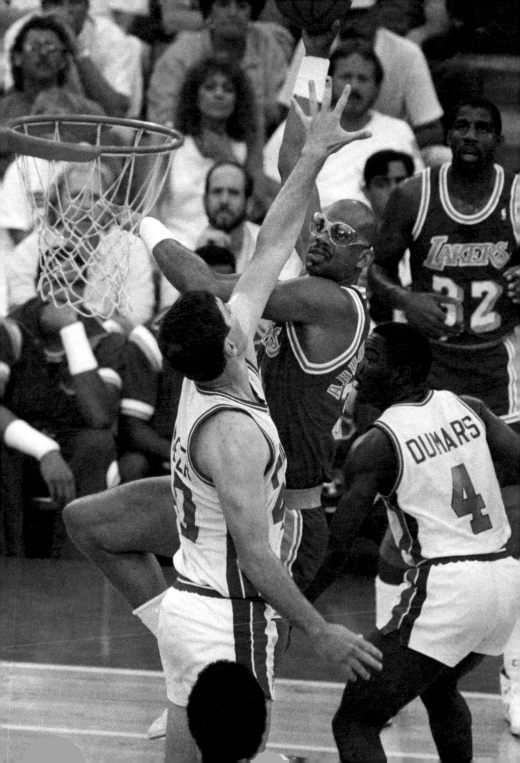

Jabbar wasn't a quitter. He sat out a few games, but then he went right back to playing his best. The Lakers, however, were swept in the tournament that season by Detroit.

A Final NBA Season

During Jabbar's final season, many wonderful things happened. A special ceremony was held at Madison Square Garden, where Coach Donohue had taken the young basketball fan when he was a high school player. He received many gifts, and he was visited by some of his old teammates from the Power Memorial Academy team. They and Coach Hopkins, who had coached him during his days at St. Jude's, were introduced to an enthusiastic crowd.

Pat Riley, who had coached Jabbar during several of his years on the Lakers, made a toast that was recounted in *Sports Illustrated*. "When a man has broken records, won championships, endured tremendous criticism and responsibility, why judge? Let's toast him as the greatest player ever." Coach

Riley put into words what many people felt in their hearts.

Other teams honored Jabbar in cities around the country, including Philadelphia, Boston, and New York. In Los Angeles, though, the celebrations of Jabbar's career were truly extraordinary. A street was even named for him!

Before the last game of the regular season, a special tribute was held. Jabbar's parents and children were there to watch as he was honored by the entire city of Los Angeles. Jabbar's teammates sang a moving tribute to him and gave him a Rolls-Royce. President George H. Bush sent a telegram. Amir, Jabbar's son, sang the national anthem. And for that last game of the season, every player wore goggles just like Jabbar's!

He had touched many people during his life, and many of them wanted to show him just how much they cared. They shouted his name during the games, and they sent him letters and gifts. They loved the way he played basketball and that he was a good person who took care of his parents and his family.

Everyone wanted Jabbar to know that they knew that he was the best. Even if he didn't always feel like he deserved their applause, he was their hero. He was, in the feelings of many, the best basketball player to ever step onto the court.

The Hall of Fame

Immediately after he retired, Jabbar completely walked away from basketball. He thought it might be forever. "I had to get away," he said in an interview in the *Houston Chronicle*. "I was totally, completely, and thoroughly burned out on the game and I had to give myself a chance to get my mind back in order."

But even if he had left basketball behind, he was not forgotten. After five seasons of retirement, his name was brought up as a Hall of Fame nominee.

No one except Jabbar had any doubt that he embodied all that is good about

The History of the Naismith Memorial Basketball Hall of Fame

The Naismith Memorial Basketball Hall of Fame is named for the college professor who invented the game. In 1891, Dr. James Naismith sought ways to encourage youngsters to exercise indoors during the winter months, after being ordered by his boss to create a indoor game in only fourteen days. Bringing outdoor games like soccer inside hadn't worked; students had been injured. With the deadline almost upon him, Dr. Naismith found some peach baskets and asked a janitor to nail them to the balconies. Then he wrote down what became the first official rules of basketball. When the Hall of Fame building was erected in 1968, it was only natural to name it after Dr. Naismith.

Dr. James Naismith

The Naismith Memorial Basketball Hall of Fame in Springfield, Massachusetts

The Hall of Fame has 238 individuals and four team inductees. Some of the individuals are players, while others are coaches, contributors, and referees. Of the 238 individuals in the Hall of Fame, 119 are players. To be eligible, a player has to have been retired for five full seasons. Then, a nomination form, a letter of support, and a packet of materials about the player, such as newspaper clippings and magazine stories, are submitted. The nominations are screened and votes are placed. Players are considered for their contributions to the sport and by how well they represented general sportsmanship and the politics of fair team play.

basketball. He told the *New York Daily News* that he was afraid he wouldn't make it in his first year of eligibility but that he was prepared to wait. "Two of my all-time heroes, Duke Snider and Willie Mays, didn't make it on the first ballot."

His father, Al, had no doubts. "He was always different, a special kid," he told the *New York Daily News*. "When he went to Power Memorial Academy, he just spread his wings and flew away. Now I can say my son made it all the way to the Hall of Fame. Did I mention how proud I am of him?"

For his own part, Jabbar gave much of the credit for his success to those he played with on the court. He told *Jet* magazine, "No one gets to this level without good teammates, and I had such tremendously good teammates." Earvin "Magic" Johnson and Oscar "the Big O" Robertson were two stars that Jabbar felt had helped him achieve his success.

Kareem Abdul-Jabbar officially became a Hall of Famer on May 15, 1995.

Life After Retirement

Although he split his time after retirement between homes in Hawaii and Los Angeles, Jabbar didn't spend his time on the beach. He had other activities to keep him busy, including working on a documentary about the African American troops who had helped liberate the Nazi death camps at the end of World War II. He also wrote four books—two autobiographies, *Black Profiles in Courage,* which was about overlooked African Americans who had accomplished great things throughout history, and *A Season on the Reservation: My Sojourn with the White Mountain Apache,* about time he had spent coaching Native American children.

Ever since Jabbar had discovered the Schomburg Center for Research in Black Culture in New York City, he had wanted to learn about the historical deeds of African Americans in the United States. He quickly realized that many who had contributed wonderful things to American history had been forgotten. He felt he could help change

that by writing a book that featured some of these people.

But he wanted to do more than write books and travel. He thought about trying to work in professional basketball, but he had been away from the NBA for more than ten years. He didn't think anyone would want to hire him after he had been away for so long.

The Buffalo Soldiers and the Apache

Finally, his attention turned toward Arizona. Some of the people Jabbar had written about in *Black Profiles in Courage* were the Buffalo Soldiers, many of whom had been stationed in Arizona, at Fort Apache. The Buffalo Soldiers were a group who had served in the Twenty-fourth and Twenty-fifth Infantry and the Tenth Cavalry. They had fought in the U.S. Army for many years along the United States–Mexican border and in the wars against Native Americans.

Jabbar was introduced to Edgar Perry, an Apache who lived on the White Mountain

Kareem Abdul-Jabbar poses at the book signing for *A Season on the Reservation* on February 7, 2000, at the NBA Store in New York City.

Reservation and whose grandfather had been a scout for the U.S. Army. Edgar helped Jabbar research the Buffalo Soldiers, including a man named John Glass, who had been stationed at Fort Apache. (Jabbar had bought a picture of Glass and wanted to know more about him, the Buffalo Soldiers, and the Apache.)

An interest in Native Americans was natural for Jabbar. His father's family, native to Trinidad, was part Caribbean Indian. His mother was part Cherokee. In actuality, Jabbar himself was one-quarter Native American. His desire to learn more about Native American cultures and the Buffalo Soldiers was a natural fascination. He listened intently and with great interest to everything Edgar Perry said and showed him.

Cora Alcindor Dies

Soon after leaving the reservation, Jabbar received terrible news. His mother, who had been very sick and in the hospital, had died. Jabbar was not surprised, but he was devastated. His

Kareem Abdul-Jabbar explains a play to members of the Falcons during a practice in 1999.

mother, Cora Alcindor, had been his first teacher. She had instilled in him a love of reading and learning and a belief that education was among the most important things in life. Jabbar credited his mother with helping him focus his will to succeed on whatever he did. She had been his first guide in life, and now she was gone.

Jabbar went to Colorado for a while and lived in a condo while he grieved over his mother's death. He thought about her life and how she was his first teacher, and he realized that he was at an age where he should be teaching youngsters the knowledge he had gained during his lifetime. Jabbar had worked with children before, even back in high school when he had gone to Friendship Farm with Coach Donohue. It was time to go back to teaching.

A Season on the Reservation

Edgar Perry visited Jabbar shortly after he returned from Colorado. Jabbar told Edgar he wanted to help kids by coaching basketball.

The very next day, Jabbar got a call from the superintendent of the White Mountain Apache school system. If Jabbar wanted, he could offer his assistance to the Alchesay High School basketball team, the Falcons, for the 1998–1999 season. Because he didn't have a teaching certificate, he would have to work as a volunteer. Jabbar jumped at the chance to work with the team.

When he arrived for his first day of practice with the team, he was amazed by how different the squad was from any he had ever been on. For one thing, the players didn't talk to each other while playing. The Falcons' game was silent. Also, the players were wild, often colliding into each other and tripping. Their shots were undisciplined and unplanned, and they couldn't dribble well. He knew that it would be hard to teach the boys the fundamentals of the game. It was possible they would not respond well to being singled out for instruction or correction.

"I want you to understand that I want to be here. I have chosen to do this with you," Jabbar recalled saying to the kids in *A Season on the Reservation.* "I hope this is a great learning experience for all of us." Although Jabbar had never been good at giving pep talks, he felt it was important to say something on his first day of coaching. He wanted the kids to know he was there not because of publicity, but to help them.

At the beginning of the season, many members of the press showed up to write about the recent Hall of Famer who was now coaching a high school team. The boys were excited to have their pictures in *Sports Illustrated*, and Jabbar was happy for them to have some attention. He hoped that their story might make other people more aware of the conditions on the reservation. Also, if colleges saw the articles, they might be more willing to welcome the youngsters into their college athletics programs.

He found that he was excited to be back on the court. Before he had been ready to get away, but now he remembered things he had liked about basketball. He enjoyed hearing the squeak of sneakers on the wooden floors, the way the players on the team talked to each other in the locker room before a game, and the smell of the ball.

He spent nearly all his time preparing practice drills and working with the team's players individually. Slowly, he got to know the youngsters. He even learned a little Apache language, too.

The children listened to Jabbar, but they didn't always use his advice on the court. He showed them standard drills, and they would work on them for a while before going back to the way they had played before. Despite the fact that he was frustrated with trying to teach the youngsters fundamentals, he was impressed with their determination and spirit.

During the first part of the season, the Falcons won three games and lost three. But in their losses, Jabbar began to see what kind of spirit the players had. In one game, they were behind because they had made mistakes. The Falcons played harder and managed to tie the score by the end. After two overtimes, the match was still tied. Jabbar got so involved in the game that he yelled at an official just like he would have done in the pros. He was afraid the official would "T" him; that is, he would call a technical foul allowing the other team two free throws and possession of the ball. In this game, that might cost the Falcons a win. The official didn't, but Jabbar's actions made the Falcons and their fans realize how much he liked them and wanted them to win.

The other team won during the third overtime, but the Falcons had proved they could play well. And Jabbar knew just how much he liked being a part of their lives. Coaching the team wasn't just something he was doing to fill his time. He was sharing his knowledge and his life with others, just as he had wanted.

Slowly, the Falcons began playing better. They learned to pass the ball well. They didn't make as many unplanned shots. Instead of running frantically around the court, they ran the plays that they had practiced.

While coaching the Falcons, Jabbar learned that he liked working with players on a one-to-one basis. He enjoyed watching them develop their style. He also valued helping them become better and more graceful athletes.

During the season, Jabbar understood more about Apache culture. He recognized the feeling of togetherness that the White Mountain Apaches had for each other, even if they weren't related. To them, everyone on the reservation was their family. Jabbar was grateful that they included him in their unit. He was even made a member of the Eagle Clan.

The Falcons lost in the state tournament, but the experience was still a good one for both Jabbar and the team. He had discovered a love for teaching and had helped the Falcons reach the state tournament when no one thought they could.

More important, though, was that Jabbar had rediscovered the love for basketball that he had put aside for a long time. He described his feelings about retirement in the introduction to his book *Black Profiles in Courage*: "It was like saying good-bye forever to someone you loved; it felt like a death. But it was also a rebirth. Because for the first time since I was eight [years old], I was free to explore my other interests." Finally, it was time to mix his love for basketball with the other interests he had explored.

When Jabbar returned to Los Angeles, he began to look for a coaching job in basketball, but he found that no one wanted to hire him after he'd spent a decade away from the game. He talked to his UCLA coach, John Wooden, but the excitement and support of the people who knew Jabbar didn't spread to those who could hire him. Not even his alma mater, UCLA, would hire him as a coach.

But then, in February 2000, the Los Angeles Clippers offered him a job as an assistant coach. Jabbar accepted. He said in an interview in the *Houston Chronicle*, "I'm in this coaching business for the long haul. I'm just happy to be here and to have been given a chance to show what I have to offer." Jabbar believed that the sport of basketball had changed, and not necessarily in a good way. "What really fueled my interest was all of the things that I see lacking in the game today. It's become a different game from the time I retired, and not a better one."

Basketball will always be a part of Jabbar's life. After a lifetime on the court, he is

Kareem Abdul-Jabbar, assistant coach for the Los Angeles Clippers, discusses a play with head coach Jim Todd during a game against the Chicago Bulls on February 19, 2000.

ready to continue teaching others the skills and the lessons that he has learned. From playing on the blacktop courts of Harlem and Inwood, to coaching at Alchesay High School, Jabbar has shown he has what it takes to be a great player, a great teacher, and a great man. Jabbar is, and will always be, one of the heroes of the sport.

glossary

agile   Able to move quickly and easily; graceful.

Allah   The supreme being of Islam.

animosity   Bitter hostility or hatred.

Arabic   The language of the Arab people. It is spoken in many Middle Eastern and African nations such as Lebanon, Syria, Iraq, and Egypt.

assist   A pass from a one player to another that leads directly to a basket.

center   Usually the tallest member on a team's starting unit; the player most responsible for plays closest to the basket, including rebounding, scoring, and shot blocking.

conviction   A strong persuasion or belief.

ethnicity   The condition of belonging to a particular nationality.

forward   One of two players flanking the
center, usually on offense. Forwards play
close to the basket, and must be good
shooters and rebounders. They are usually
taller than guards, but shorter than centers.

free throw   An uncontested shot, worth one
point, taken by a player who has been
fouled. The number of shots depend on the
situation of the foul. Also called a foul shot.

Islam   The religious faith of Muslims, which
includes belief in Allah as the sole deity
and in Muhammad as his prophet.

Mecca   City in Saudi Arabia; the birthplace
of Muhammad and holy city of Islam.

monotheism   A belief in one God.

mosque   A building used for public worship
by Muslims.

Muhammad   The Islamic prophet who
delivered the religious stories that make up
the Qur'an.

Muslim   A follower of Islam.

Qur'an   A book composed of sacred writings
accepted by Muslims as revelations made

to Muhammad by Allah through the angel Gabriel.

racism   A belief that race is the primary determinant of human traits and that racial differences produce an ultimate superiority of a particular race.

rebound   To retrieve the ball as it comes from the rim or backboard, taking possession of it for either team.

Sabbath   A day of rest and worship.

veteran   A person of long experience in some occupation or skill.

for more information

ESPN TV and Radio
ESPN Plaza
Bristol, CT 06010
http://www.espn.com

Naismith Memorial Basketball Hall of Fame
1150 West Columbus Avenue
Springfield, MA 01105
(413) 781-6500
(877) 4HOOPLA (446-6752)
Web sites: http://www.hoophall.com
http://www.basketballhalloffame.com

National Basketball Association (NBA)
645 Fifth Avenue
New York, NY 10022
http://www.nba.com

Abdul-Jabbar, Kareem. *A Champion Strategy.* New York: William Morrow & Co., 2001.

Abdul-Jabbar, Kareem, and Alan Steinberg. *Black Profiles in Courage.* New York: Avon Books, 2000.

Abdul-Jabbar, Kareem, and Peter Knobler. *Giant Steps.* New York: Bantam Books, 1985.

Abdul-Jabbar, Kareem, and Mignon McCarthy. *Kareem.* New York: Random House, 1990.

Abdul-Jabbar, Kareem, and Stephen Singular. *A Season on the Reservation: My Sojourn with the White Mountain Apache.* New York: William Morrow and Co., 2000.

Borrello, Helen A. *Kareem Abdul-Jabbar: Basketball Legends.* New York: Chelsea House Publishers, 1995.

Cobourn, R. Thomas. *Kareem Abdul-Jabbar: Basketball Great* (Black Americans of Achievement). New York: Chelsea House Publishers, 1995.

Howard-Cooper, Scott. *The Bruin 100: The Greatest Games in the History of UCLA Basketball*. Lenexa, KS: The Addax Publishing Group, 1999.

index

About the Author

Martha Kneib is a native St. Louisan who returned to her hometown after finishing her master's degree in anthropology in 1990. She immediately began trying to break into a professional writing career and since 1991 has, under the name Marella Sands, sold two historical novels, several short stories, nonfiction articles, and has coauthored several books. She devotes most of her time to writing, maintaining her Web sites, and planning vacations to fascinating places.

Photo Credits

Cover © Corbis; pp. 4, 53 © Sporting News/Archive Photos; pp. 8, 18–19, 24, 28–29, 33, 35, 40–41, 56–57, 72, 81 © Corbis; p. 24 © courtesy of the Schomburg Center for Research in Black Culture; p. 43 © Reuters/Abbas Monumani/Archive Photos; pp. 46, 76–77 © Everett Collection; pp. 13, 50, 61, 86, 87, 90, 100 © AP/Wide World Photos; p. 63 © New York Times Co./Ernest Sisto/Archive Photos; p. 93 © Robert Harbison/1999 The Christian Science Monitor.

Series Design and Layout

Geri Giordano